MY FIRST DUCK HUNT!

Written by
Beverly King

Illustrated by
Bex Sutton

Published by
Beverly's Children's Books
Illustrated by Bex Sutton
Edited by Nay Merrill
Copyright @ 2022 by Beverly King

Paperback: 978-1-7353836-8-2
Hardback: 978-1-7353836-9-9

Dedicated To

This book is dedicated to all the ethical hunters out there! You are making an actual difference while being responsible. Continue to share what ethical hunting means so we may continue to hunt for generations to come.

Special thank you to my friend Joanna Tjaden, my sisters-in-law, Cindy King and Kathy Gau, my daughter, Sierra King, and to my mom, Mary Stewart, for their valuable suggestions along the way.

beverlyschildrensbooks@gmail.com

beverlyschildrensbooks.com

My mom woke me up early Monday morning and said,
"Rise and shine! Breakfast is on the table."
I smiled at her, **excited** for the day ahead.

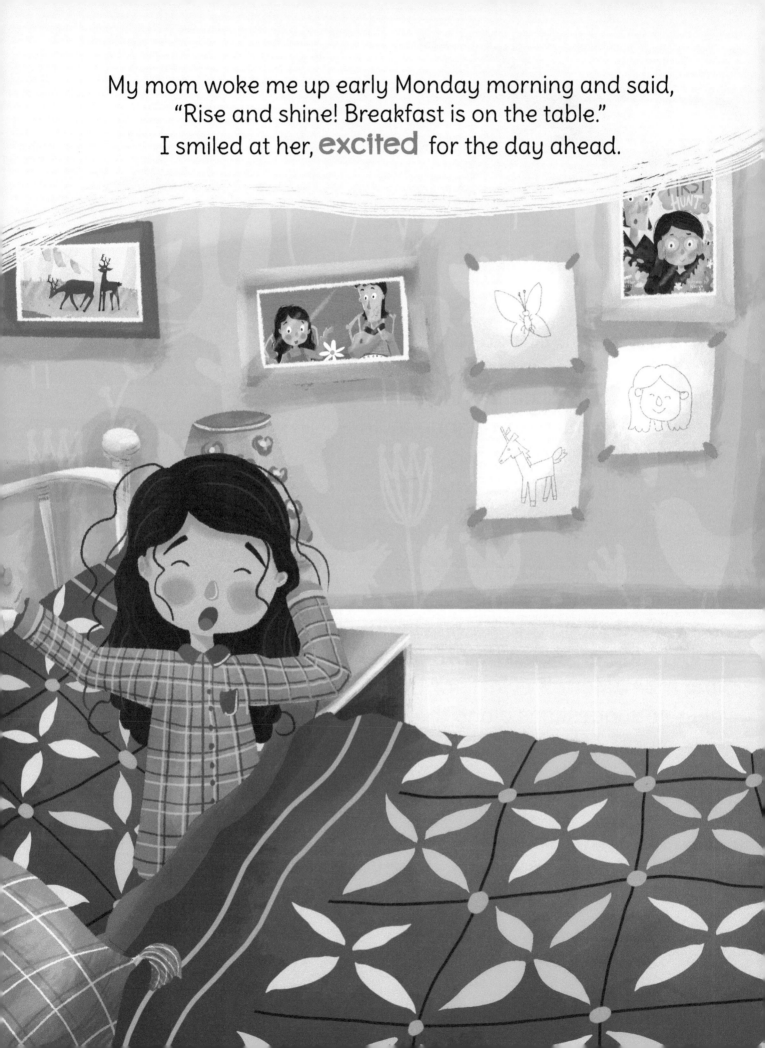

Today was a **special** day!

I had been **dreaming** about it for as long as I could remember.

Today, my mom and I were going duck hunting!

During the spring, I completed my hunter's safety course.

I learned how to be a **responsible** and **ethical** hunter and how to carry and shoot a shotgun safely.

We went over how to look for different types of birds flying above.

You legally can not shoot just anything flying above you.

Each bird has their season, and to be an ethical hunter, you need to know the difference between males and females and the types of birds.

I have watched my mom work with Jessie, our Labrador retriever, teaching her different commands that she would need to know to do her job as a retriever.

Once I was old enough to get my license, my mom and I practiced shooting clay pigeons at the local range to get ready for duck season.

Shooting the clay pigeons helped me learn how to lift the shotgun while aiming at a moving target overhead.

With excitement for the day ahead,
I threw off my covers and jumped
out of bed. I grabbed my
hunting camos and
my waders, along with
Jessie's vest.

When Jessie saw her vest in my hands, she started turning circles with excitement as she knew what this meant. It meant she was going duck hunting.

Jessie loves to go duck hunting. She has a job of retrieving the birds after being shot and then bringing them to us.

Once I got washed up, we headed to the kitchen for breakfast.

During breakfast, my mom said, "This will be a great day to hunt, the fog has lifted and the wind has died down."

NEWS

When breakfast was over, we loaded up the truck and headed towards the river as the **full moon** shone above us.

During the drive, my mom told me the story of her first duck hunt. Her dad had a secret spot they would go to, and it would be just them with no one else around for miles.

I smiled and listened as my mom also smiled while talking about how much she learned about hunting from her parents and grandparents.

On my mom's first duck hunt, she filled her limit with mallards and widgeons while taking a clean shot each time.

My mom reminded me that taking a clean shot is an essential requirement to take home any animal ethically. Ducks are beautiful animals and deserve our respect. If you can not take a clean shot, you must wait for the next ducks to fly over. As I listened to my mom, I got excited, wondering how my first duck hunt would go.

Once we arrived at a clear spot near the river, we unloaded the truck and grabbed our gear, ensuring the ammunition was secure and the gun's safety was on. Jessie ran alongside us as we walked towards the water.

Along the way, we saw cattails, bulrush, and sedges as the moon shone down on us.

Once at the edge of the water, my mom set
out the decoys to help attract the ducks,
then we got settled into a spot.

As the sun rose above, we saw song sparrows, red-winged blackbirds, and northern flickers.

As the sun rose higher, we saw a pair of bald eagles perched on a branch on a tall tree, and off in the distance in the water, we saw great blue herons, ring-billed gulls, and some belted kingfishers.

Then my mom spotted ducks flying in the distance. She told me to get ready as she blew into the duck call.

As the ducks started to approach overhead, we saw they were mallards. My mom blew in the duck call once again, and they headed our way.

My mom asked if I was ready. I nodded my head with excitement.

Then I took a deep breath and raised my shotgun. My mom said, "Shoot when ready."

I took another deep breath as I took off the safety, followed a duck above, and pulled the trigger.

"Nice shot, Sierra!" my mom yelled as she gave Jessie the command to retrieve the duck.

Jessie returned with the duck in her mouth, then dropped it at my feet. "Good girl," my mom said as Jessie wagged her tail.

As I looked down at the duck, my heart sank with sadness. I just shot a beautiful bird, and now it lay lifeless at my feet.

We continued to hunt until we had our limit. Then we gave our thanks as we bowed our heads with gratitude.

Then we packed up our gear and headed back to the truck with Jessie leading the way.

Back at the truck, my mom called my grandma and gave her the news.

After loading up the truck with all our gear, we headed back home.

Once home, we unloaded the truck and put the ducks in the garage sink to be de-feathered and washed.

We set some aside for dinner, and the rest we put in the freezer for another day.

I was excited for dinner as we were making my grandpa's favorite dish.

Duck fajitas!

My grandma had a recipe that made the duck taste amazing.

We washed up and got ready for a late lunch. Over lunch, my grandma asked me how my morning went. I smiled proudly as I talked about where we went and what we saw.

I talked about all the excitement that went through my head, along with the sadness I felt after my first shot. My mom and grandma smiled while they listened to me talk about our morning as I told my first duck hunting story.

Glossary

Cattails

Cattail is a slender perennial, aquatic, emergent plant, growing to 1.5 – 2 meters tall. They can help minimize bank erosion on steep or wind-swept shorelines. Cattails play a vital role in the wild as they are a source of food and shelter for various birds and mammals.

Bulrushes

Bulrushes grow in wet locations, including ponds, marshes, and lakes. Their stems are often used to weave strong mats, baskets, and chair seats.

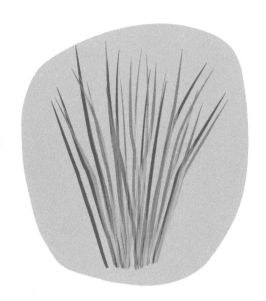

Sedges

Sedges are one of the largest groups of plants with over 2,000 species. Sedges are found in almost every part of the world, and they thrive in different growing conditions. You can find sedges in the sun or shade and in dry or moist conditions. Sedge plants produce tiny seeds that feed some bird species, and many animals use the foliage to line and create nests.

Song Sparrow

One of the most widespread sparrows in North America. Reasonably large with a long, rounded tail. Overall coarsest patterned with gray and brown, usually with more reddish-brown wings and tail. Found in various scrubby habitats both near and far from human development, especially edges of fields, often near water.

Bald Eagles

The bald eagle's range includes Canada, the United States, and northern Mexico. Found near sizeable open water bodies with an abundant food supply and old-growth trees for nesting.

Red-winged blackbird

One of the most abundant birds across North America and one of the most boldly colored, the red-winged blackbird is a familiar sight atop cattails, along soggy roadsides, and on telephone wires. Glossy-black males have scarlet-and-yellow shoulder patches they can puff up or hide, depending on how confident they feel. Females are a subdued, streaky brown, almost like a large, dark sparrow. Their early and tumbling song are happy indications of the return of spring.

Great blue heron

The great blue heron is the largest heron species in North America, standing about 4 feet tall. But even though they are large birds, they don't weigh much (only 5 to 6 pounds), thanks to their light, hollow bones (a trait most birds have). Nests vary widely. A first-time nest maybe only 20 inches across. Other nests used repeatedly for many years can reach 4 feet in diameter and be nearly as deep. A great blue heron colony might have more than 500 nests. For such large and lanky birds, herons are speedy, flying as fast as 30 mph. With a lightning-fast strike, herons quickly catch fish or frogs as a meal.

Northern Flickers

Flickers are relatively large woodpeckers with a slim, rounded head, slightly down-curved bill, and long flared tail that tapers to a point. Flickers appear brownish overall, with a white rump patch conspicuous in flight and often visible when perched. The undersides of the wing and tail feathers are bright yellow in eastern birds or red in western birds. You'll see the brown plumage richly patterned with black spots, bars, and crescents with a closer look.

Ring-billed gulls

Ring-billed gulls forage in flight or pick up objects while swimming, walking, or wadding. They also steal food from other birds and frequently scavenge. They are omnivores; their diet may include insects, fish, grain, eggs, earthworms, and rodents. Their habitat is near lakes, rivers, or the coast in Canada or the northern United States.

Belted kingfisher

The belted kingfisher is often apparent from its wild rattling call while it flies over lakes or rivers. They are often seen perched high on a snag or hovering while it beats its wings rapidly before plunging headfirst into the water to grab a fish. It is found throughout almost all of North America in one season or another and is the only member of the kingfisher family to be found in most areas to the north of Mexico.

Mallard

The male mallard duck, called a drake, sports a glossy-green head, a white ring around its neck, and a rich chestnut-brown breast. The mottled brown female mallard looks downright dull next to the male's showy feathers. You'll find mallard ducks near ponds, marshes, streams, and lakes, where they feed on plants, fish, and insects.

Widgeons

The American wigeon is often the fifth most commonly harvested duck in the United States, behind the mallard, green-winged teal, gadwall, and wood duck. The American wigeon is a bird of open wetlands, such as wet grasslands or marshes with taller vegetation. They usually feed by dabbling for plant food or grazing, which it does very readily.

Spot 12 differences

Questions

1. Why is hunting necessary?

2. Do you need to take hunter safety education?

3. What does hunting mean to you?

4. Do all ducks get hunted?

5. What is a duck stamp?

6. What is gun safety?

One of the most anticipated days of the year for one young girl. The day when everything changes and a young girl's father tells her she is ready. Ready for the great hunt.

She used to just watch as her dad hunts, this time will be different. This time the young girl has her own hunting license and will be hunting. Join our young adventurer as she and her father explore the terrain, searching for scat and tracks in hopes to find the right deer for hunting.

This beautifully illustrated children's book is a perfect read about hunting for beginners and a fantastic family bonding book. Not just a story about outdoor activities for families, this tale follows this father and daughter duo whilst they explore the importance and perils of hunting and how it affects nature's ecosystem.

Available on Amazon